This Journal Belongs To:

____

Made in the USA
Columbia, SC
05 June 2024

36654782R00074